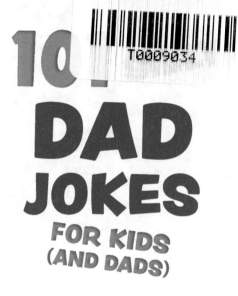

101
DAD
JOKES
FOR KIDS
(AND DADS)

T0009034

101 SILLY DAD JOKES

FOR KIDS (AND DADS)

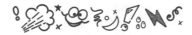

Jess Kiddin

ULYSSES BOOKS
FOR YOUNG READERS

Published by:
Ulysses Books for Young Readers,
an imprint of Ulysses Press
PO Box 3440
Berkeley, CA 94703

ISBN: 978-1-64604-669-0
Library of Congress Control Number: 2024931679

Printed in the United States
2 4 6 8 10 9 7 5 3 1

Image credits from shutterstock: cover © Vector
Illusion; interior © HobbitArt (top), © Shannon Marie
Baldwin (bottom)

What kind of tree fits in your hand?

A palm tree!

What did one plate say to the other plate?

Lunch is on me!

**What did the grape
say when it got
stepped on?**

Nothing, it just let
out a little whine!

What do you call a sleeping bull?

A bulldozer.

Why don't oysters donate to charity?

Because they are shellfish.

Why was the broom always late?

It over-swept.

What do you call fake spaghetti?

An "impasta."

Why was the computer cold?

It left its Windows open.

Why did the scarecrow go to school?

He wanted to be outstanding in a field.

What do you get
when you cross a
snake with a pie?

A python.

Why did the boy bring a ladder to school?

He wanted to go to high school.

Why did the chicken join a band?

Because it had a pair of drumsticks.

What do you call a pile of kittens?

A meowtain.

Why do bees have sticky hair?

Because they use honeycombs.

What do you call a
bear without ears?

B!

What's orange and sounds like a parrot?

A carrot.

What has keys but opens no locks?

A piano.

How do you fix a broken tomato?

Tomato paste.

What do you call a fish in a tuxedo?

So-fish-ticated.

Why did the girl smear peanut butter on the road?

To go with the traffic jam.

What's a tree's favorite school subject?

Geome-tree.

What do you call a bear with no socks on?

Bare-foot.

What do you call a sheep with no head and no legs?

A cloud.

Why did the teddy bear say no to dessert?

Because it was stuffed.

**Why did the boy
throw his watch out
of the window?**

He wanted to see time fly.

How do you make an octopus laugh?

With ten-tickles.

Why did the cow give only buttermilk?

Because it couldn't churn the other cheek.

How do you communicate with a fish?

Drop it a line!

What did the fisherman say to the magician?

Pick a cod, any cod!

What do you call a dinosaur with an extensive vocabulary?

A thesaurus!

What did one hat say to the other?

You stay here; I'll go on ahead!

What's a tree's favorite drink?

Root beer!

Why do bananas have to put on sunscreen before they go to the beach?

So they don't peel!

What's a vampire's favorite fruit?

A blood orange!

How do you make a milk shake?

Give a cow a pogo stick!

Why did the banana go to the doctor?

It wasn't peeling well.

Why couldn't the leopard play hide and seek?

He was always spotted!

Why did the football team go to the bank?

To get their quarterback.

Why did the student eat his homework?

Because his teacher said it was a piece of cake!

What's a witch's favorite class in school?

Spelling!

What do you call a bear that's always cold?

A polar bear.

What did the little corn say to the mama corn?

Where's popcorn?

What do you call a lazy kangaroo?

A pouch potato.

What's a pirate's favorite letter?

Arrrrr!

Why did the duck get detention?

For making her friends quack up during class.

Why did the chicken sit on an egg?

It didn't have a chair!

How does the moon cut her hair?

Sh-eclipse it!

What did the Dalmatian say after lunch?

"That hit the spot!"

How do you invite
a British dinosaur
to lunch?

"Tea, Rex?"

What do you call a pig that knows karate?

Pork chop!

How do you make
an egg giggle?

Tell it a yolk!

Why don't eggs tell each other funny stories?

Because they might crack up!

What do you call a rabbit with fleas?

Bugs Bunny.

What is a dog magician's favorite spell?

"Labracadabrador!"

Why did the orange stop in the middle of the road?

It ran out of juice.

My dog is great at math. When you offer him a treat, he's all ears plus tail!

I'm reading a book on anti-gravity. It's impossible to put down!

I'd tell you the construction joke, but I'm still working on it.

If you see a crime at an Apple Store, does that make you an iWitness?

I'd tell you a joke about time travel, but you didn't like it.

When I told my dad to act his age, he suddenly became extinct!

I became a
baker because I
kneaded dough.

The math teacher called my friend average. How mean!

Why doesn't the comedian tell jokes about herbs?

She said it's too thyme-consuming.

**I couldn't remember
how to throw a
boomerang, but then
it came back to me!**

**Knock, knock.
Who's there?
Lettuce.
Lettuce who?**

**Lettuce in, it's
cold out here!**

Knock, knock.
Who's there?
Boo.
Boo who?

Don't cry, it's just a joke!

Knock, knock.
Who's there?
Atch.
Atch who?

Bless you!

Knock, knock.
Who's there?
Harry.
Harry who?

Harry up and
answer the door!

**Knock, knock.
Who's there?
Interrupting cow.
Interrup...**

MOO!

Knock, knock.
Who's there?
Broken pencil.
Broken pencil who?

Never mind, it's point-less.

**Knock, knock.
Who's there?
Canoe.
Canoe who?**

**Canoe unlock this door
I forgot my key?**

Knock, knock.
Who's there?
Woo.
Woo who?

Woo hoo! It's the weekend!

Knock, knock.
Who's there?
Dishes.
Dishes who?

Dishes a really good joke!

Add Your Own Jokes!

_____

_____

_____

_____

_____

_____

_____

_____

_____

_____

_____

_____

_____